Youtube Success

The Ultimate Guide to Starting a YouTube Channel for Beginners

By

Anuranjan Vikas

Introduction

Hi guys, Thanks for stopping by to buy this book. So, what is this book about??Who is it for?? How is it useful?? Lets see..

Do you want a passive income?

Are you a student who wants extra pocket money?

Do you want to earn money entertaining people?

Do you want to earn money while doing what you like??

Then this book is for you!! (even if you don't fit into any of the above question)

Youtube Success: The Ultimate guide to starting a youtube channel for beginners is a simple buy useful guide for anyone of any age who wants to kick start there youtube career. So, without further delay lets jump into the world of fun and entertainment!!

Table of Contents

If you're doing any kind of business online, making the decision to be on YouTube is an easy one.

- YouTube is the second largest search engine (it's Daddy, Google, is number one)
- If you have video on your website, you're 53x more likely to show up in Google search
- 52% of consumers who watch product videos say they are more confident about purchasing them.

And here's the kicker...YouTube is free to use and the only thing you absolutely need to get started aside from an internet connection is a smartphone.

Yes, there are many products, tools, tips, and tricks that you can add to your arsenal as you grow (and we'll get to those), but when you're starting from scratch, done is better than perfect, and if you're not taking advantage of YouTube yet in 2015, there's no time to waste.

Let's get started.

Define the Purpose of Your Channel

The reasons to be on YouTube are obvious, but before you get started, it's important to define the purpose of your YouTube channel.

- Maybe you have an existing business and you want to inform customers about your products by creating how-to videos to help your customers and reach new ones.
- Maybe you're a musician and you want your music to reach a bigger audience to help sell more tickets and merchandise.
- Maybe you are an individual wanting to indulge in a hobby, using YouTube as an avenue to meet more people in a like-minded community and make a little extra cash to help pay for your passion.
- Maybe you want to review gadgets, games or toys and grow a channel big enough that it allows you to quit your job and create videos full time.
- Maybe you are inspired by the personalities of one or more popular YouTubers and want to put yourself out there with the hopes of becoming one of the world's highest paid YouTube stars.

Maybe at this point, you simply have a passion for creating videos and need help nailing down a niche idea for your new channel.

If that's you, here's 30 YouTube channel ideas to help you out:

Regardless of what niche you choose, defining the purpose of your YouTube channel and having a clear vision of what it is you want to achieve will not only help you choose what type of content to create but it will also help keep you on track when you get tired, lose patience, or run into obstacles along the way. Knowing where you want to go makes it a lot easier to clear a path that will take you there.

Ask yourself the following 5 questions to help define the purpose of your YouTube Channel:

1. Why do you want to start a YouTube Channel?
   Be as detailed as possible. No vague answers.
   For example, "to go viral and get rich" is NOT a valid answer and will get you nowhere fast.
2. What will you make videos about and do you have a genuine interest in this niche?
   Whether you're starting a YouTube channel as new venture or as an additional marketing tool for an exciting business, Creating videos and building a channel is a lot of work and dedication, you need to have an interest in the type of content you are creating. If you're immersed in a subject you do not have any interest in, it will be 10x harder than if it was a topic you genuinely enjoyed.
3. Are there other YouTubers serving this niche...successfully?
   A big misconception when people are choosing whether or not to pursue a niche topic (or a type of marketing video for their business) is that if there are lots of people doing it, then it's a bad idea to pursue it themselves. This couldn't be further from the truth, especially if it is a big audience with a lot of problems to be solved and needs you can fulfill. Instead of worrying about "over-saturation" and "too much competition", try to find ways you can add your own twist on what they're doing. What can you add that they are not? What holes can you fill that they have left behind?
4. How much time (and patience) do you have?
   You must be willing to sacrifice the time it takes to achieve the growth of a new YouTube channel. Unless you already have an audience that can be sent to your new venture, building a successful YouTube channel takes time. Period. Yes, it varies, and there have been overnight sensations, but the tried and tested road to longevity is the willingness to put in the sweat equity for months, or even years, depending on what your ultimate goals are.
5. How will you measure your success?
   Defining success is huge. Similar to the first question, being as detailed here as possible will go a long way in helping you succeed. Setting milestones and short term goals as well as the

bigger long term ones will help you stay on track. Do you want to make x-amount of sales, get x-amount of subscribers, get x-amount of views, meet x-amount of people, make x-amount of Adsense money? Write it all down so you are clear on where you're going. Then, get started on the steps that will take you there.

Ok, time to take the answers to these questions and put them into action.

Set Up Your New YouTube Channel in 3 Easy Steps

Now that you know the purpose of your channel and the type of content you're going to create, the next step is the initial set up process. Luckily, starting a new YouTube channel is free and relatively easy to do.

Since YouTube is a service provided by Google, you are going to need to have an existing Google account. If you do not already have one, just go to accounts.google.com, create an account, and then head over to YouTube.com, login with your account info, and continue reading.

Step 1: Create Your YouTube Channel Account

Now that you're logged in to YouTube, you will see the main menu on the top left of the page.

Click on "My Channel" to get started.

This will pop up a dialog box where you can choose to create a channel using your personal name or a business name.

If you want to use your personal name, simply fill it in and click "create channel".

If you want to choose a business name, click the text in this box that reads "Use a business or other name".

If you chose to use a business name, you will be taken to the following window. Enter your business name, select the type of business, agree to the terms by checking the box, and then click "Done".

Tips on Choosing a Great YouTube Channel Name

If you're not going to use your personal name and you don't have an existing business or an obvious name to use already, sometimes it can cause a little anxiety having to choose one. It's understandable, it's a serious commitment.

Just relax and take these things into consideration when choosing a name:

- Is it relevant to your the video content you will be providing on your channel?
- Does it provide flexibility? A specific targeted niche is great, but it's a also a good idea to leave yourself room to expand and branch out a little bit in the future, so just be sure your name doesn't leave you stuck in a way that new video topics would fit.
- Easy to remember and short as possible
- The exact name is available on YouTube and other social platforms for continuity across all social media. This isn't 100% necessary, but definitely is a bonus for branding purposes.

Need more help? Try a YouTube name generator.

Step 2: Upload Your Channel Art (and Icon)

Now that you've officially created your new channel, you'll want to customize it with personal and/or branded images. YouTube refers to the main header image as "channel art" and calls the profile square image in the top left the "channel icon".

Your YouTube channel art image should be 2560 x 1440 pixels and will not be accepted if the file size exceeds 4MB.

The reason your channel art is so big is so it will cover the screen area of any device including TVs as you can see in the screenshot example below.

Channel Art Tips

Notice that there is quite a big difference in the amount of visible area of your image across different devices? It's important to keep any important info near the center of the image to be sure it is seen by all users regardless of which device they are using.

Want more than just your logo on your channel art but unsure how to tackle the design yourself?

Here are 3 ways to help you get an elaborate channel art design created while saving you the headache of having to figure out all the size dimensions, safe areas, and other design intricacies on your own.

- Use this free YouTube channel art template (this will provide the guidelines necessary to keep your important elements within the safe areas.)
- Buy a channel art design template for a few bucks. (these are more elaborate "done for you" design templates where you can easily edit in your own text and images while keeping the same overall design)
- Order a custom channel art design (Fiverr is a great value for hiring people to do creative tasks like this)

Step 3: Add Your Channel Description and Other Details

Now that you've got your channel art in order, it's time to tell your audience what they can expect from you by filling in the "About" section with a description of you, your channel, and it's content.

You can easily do this by clicking the "About" link on your channel menu bar.

This will open the About page and allow you to write a description about you and your channel, up to 1,000 words in length.

While you're on this page, you can also enter a contact email (for business inquiries), choose your country, and add up to 5 links that will appear on the bottom right of your channel art at the top of the page.

When you add links to appear on your channel, you can choose to have the title appear on any custom links that you add (up to 30 characters). This is a good place to add a link to your website as well as any other social profiles you have.

When you add profiles like Twitter, Facebook, etc. YouTube automatically adds the social icons as links in the bottom right of the channel art.

Ok, Time to Verify Your YouTube Channel

Now that you have the basics of your YouTube channel setup complete, the final step of this initial set up is to verify your YouTube channel.

The reason you want to verify your channel is this gives you access to many of the added features that you definitely want to take advantage of, like custom thumbnails, the ability to upload longer videos. content ID disputes, external annotations, and more.

It's quick and easy to verify. While logged in, simply go to http://youtube.com/features and from there, at the top of the page you will see the "Verify" button. Click it, and choose which way you would like to verify (phone or text)

Here's a quick video walkthrough of how to verify your channel:

PHEW! You did it! You have officially completed the initial setup of your new YouTube channel...Congrats!

How to Create Videos That Your Audience Wants to Watch

Since you're just starting your new YouTube channel, you're probably so excited that your head is spinning out of control with fresh video ideas for your channel.

That's great, but before you spend all the time and effort it takes to create, edit, and upload a video, it's a good idea to do a little research first to make sure that your video idea is one that your audience actually wants to watch.

How do you do that?

Use Google to Find Out Exactly What Videos You Should Create for Your Audience

Google has a few easy to use tools that will blatantly tell you what your audience is watching and/or searching for. Use these tools to ensure you're on the right track with creating videos people want to watch.

Instant Search Results (predictive search) - You have probably seen this in action before. It's when Google shows you search queries as you start typing a sentence like this:

What are these results exactly? Google defines them as follows:

The possible searches that you see are based on what other people are searching for and the content of web pages indexed by Google.

SerpStat - This quick and easy tool takes Google's instant Search Results to a whole new level. You can enter your base keyword and get a ton of detailed search queries to use for video ideas in seconds. The "Only questions" filter is an amazing feature.

Google Trends - Learning to use Google Trends can be an extremely effective way to create super-targeted content that will help you get extra views while the topic is hot and trending.

What's Already Working on YouTube for Others?

Part of your idea research routine should be searching what has already been working for others in your niche on YouTube. The idea is not to copy them, but to discover what it is that your audience is the most interesting in seeing.

Use the YouTube search filters to "sort by upload date" to get the latest results from this year or even the past month so you're seeing the what works most recently.

It's also a good idea to filter by "view count". Sometimes, you'll get videos with inflated views just because it's a popular channel, but here's where you can take it a step further. If videos has a 10s of thousands of views, that usually also means there's a ton of comments. Sift through the comments and see if you can find common questions or concerns. What did the creator leave out of this popular video that you can capitalize on in yours?

Just because you think "photos of leg warners on giraffes" are awesome, it doesn't mean your audience will. Do the research so you don't end up with videos on your channel that only have 3 views (all from you).

How to Create the Best Video Quality for YouTube Without Breaking the Bank

Now that you have a list of video ideas that you know your audience wants to watch, it's time to get to the fun part -- making the videos!

What equipment to use to create videos on YouTube is probably one of the most popular questions on YouTube itself. Since you're just getting started, and probably don't want to spend a ton of money on equipment before you even have your first video uploaded, this will be a basic rundown of options that you have to increase the quality of video and sound without breaking the bank.

Here are the basic needs to get you started:

The Camera (Video)

Unless you're strictly making screencast videos, you're going to need a camera to record video. There are entire websites dedicated to video camera equipment reviews and tutorials on how to use it all, but right now, you only need to focus on the bear necessities. There's no need to be overwhelmed with choosing a camera, when you likely already have something that's perfectly fine to get you started.

Here are your choices:

Smartphone

Most people have everything they need for shooting quality video in their smartphone, especially the newer models.

There are even a few benefits to using your smartphone to record your videos for YouTube. It's usually always with you, you can share videos to YouTube quickly and easily, and there are a number of apps that can help you with organizing, editing, and adding effects to your videos.

There are a couple of downsides as well though that you need to be aware of.

- The audio will likely low quality and/or noisy, especially if recording outside.
- Video stabilization can be a problem, depending on the type of videos you're making.

There are relatively cheap ways to remedy these issues though and get an even better quality video recording from your smartphone.

If you're going to use your smartphone and want to drastically improve your audio, a Lavalier microphone like the Rode smartLav+ is a great choice.

To fix the stabilization issue that you might have with your smartphone, the JOBY GripTight GorillaPod is a really cool, and functional option for under $15! It can be used to creatively secure your camera in different settings as well, like a tree for example (the tripod securely wraps tightly around objects)

Webcam

If you use a laptop, chances are there's a webcam built in. While these don't typically have the best quality, some are very good, especially the ones built into the newer Macs. If you have good lighting, it can do the trick for many types of videos and similar to using a smartphone, it can be convenient if you're used to always being in front of the computer.

This webcam has a high number of excellent customer reviews and although it is best suited for Windows, it also works with Mac. If a webcam is up your alley, then the Logitech HD Pro Webcam C920 is probably one of the best choices, especially on a budget.

DSLR or Camcorder

You may already have a DSLR camera or camcorder at home that you use for family vacations, etc. This is the most expensive option, and will take some research on your part if you want to buy one, as you will have many questions when trying to make the choice between a DSLR vs. a camcorder.

The upside of the extra expense is that the quality is amazing, especially if you have a good lens.

The Microphone (Audio)

You CAN create videos with the built in microphone of whatever device you choose, but the difference of an external microphone is literally about 10 quality levels higher, and that's just with the relatively inexpensive ones. You simply can't get high quality sound from the built in mics (unless you export the audio separately and fiddle with it using a sound editing program, but who's got time for that?)

If you're on a strict budget, then you can go without one until you can get a microphone, but that should be one of your top priorities for equipment moving forward.

That being said, getting an external mic doesn't have to be too painful. Here are a few options to choose from:

If you're looking for a decent clip style mic that you can just hide near your shirt collar, theSony ECMCS3 is well worth it's enticing cost of under $20.

Are you going to be sitting at a desk, or using your built-in webcam but need high quality audio? For the price, the Audio-Technica AT2020 USB Cardioid Condenser Mic rivals many others that are 3x it's cost.

If you're looking for an external mic for your DSLR, there doesn't get much better than Rode and the Rode VMGO Shotgun Mic is excellent for the price. It also doesn't need a battery like many others and runs off plugin-power. PLUS, it has a built in shock mount!

The Lighting

if you're able to constantly shoot your videos during the day, in a well-lit room with natural light beaming into the perfect spot where you're shooting, then you might be able to get away with not having lights. However, even with the best conditions, it's highly unlikely that your circumstances will be perfect all of the times you want to record.

The best scenario on a minimal budget is to have two soft lights on either side of the camera pointing at you.

There are some pretty decent lighting kits available at a fairly low cost that will elevate your video quality.

For under $60, the CowboyStudio Photography & Video Portrait Umbrella Continuous Triple Lighting Kit is a steal and while it's not the most professional lighting kit, it will definitely help make your videos look way more professional.

This is a similar kit but with soft boxes and a boom stand so you can have a top light above you, which takes the lighting up another level. CowboyStudio 2275 Watt Digital Video Continuous Softbox Lighting Kit with Boom and Carrying Case

Watch the video below to see a couple of fairly inexpensive lights in action. The set up being used here is comparative in price to the suggestions above but allows you a bit more lighting control. They also require less room and would be easier to store and pack up to take to different locations if that matters to you. The downside is they use batteries and that can be a hassle sometimes.

The Editing Software

WAIT! Do not panic! Many first time video creators get a little nervous and overwhelmed when they see all the different options for editing software, and if that wasn't enough, they have to then figure out how to USE the one they choose!

It's not as hard as it seems. In fact, some of the free software out there is extremely intuitive and easy to use for YouTube newbs.

Derral Eves does an excellent job (in under 8 minutes) breaking down the different editing software available, from the free ones for beginners to the premium ones for pros. There are options for both for Mac and PC users.

Optimizing Your YouTube Channel to Get More Views and Subscribers

Once you have video content on your YouTube channel, you will want to optimize your channel to ensure that as many people are seeing your videos as possible.

Here are a few of the most important optimizing strategies to get you started.

The Trailer

You might have noticed that when you arrive at the home page of a YouTube channel you are not subscribed to, you will see a highlighted video near the top of the page that auto-plays when the channel page loads. That is a trailer video.

The trailer video will only appear for viewers who have not yet subscribed to your channel. This is an excellent way to quickly show your visitors what your channel is all about and explain to them why it is a good idea for them to subscribe.

YouTube provides great advice on creating a channel trailer for new viewers:

Assume the viewer has never heard of you.

- Keep it short.
- Hook your viewers in the first few seconds.
- Show, don't tell.
- Ask viewers to subscribe in your video and with annotations.

Organize Your Content Using Sections and Playlists

YouTube allows you some control over your channel page layout in the form of sections and playlists.

It's pretty simple, but extremely effective. It gives viewers an instant organized overview of all the different types of content your channel provides at a glance.

Sections

Adding a section is easy. While logged into your YouTube account, scroll to the bottom of your channel home page and click the button that reads "add a section"

Now you will see two dropdown menus that allow you to choose what type of content you want to show in this new section and also whether you'd like it to appear horizontal or vertical.

Playlists

Playlists are a great way to organize related videos on your channel, but they also help encourage viewers to spend more time on your channel by listing all of your playlists' videos on the sidebar of the playlist window.

This is extremely helpful now that YouTube's top search ranking factor is watch time and not just subscribers and views.

Create Custom Eye-Catching Thumbnails

Amy Schmittauer from Savvy Sexy Social calls YouTube thumbnails "Human SEO".

What she means by that it is, when you create a custom thumbnail, opposed to letting YouTube just choose one for you (which is just a random screenshot), you are increasing the chances of "winning" the clickthrough over the competition.

Here are a few more tips for creating your custom thumbnail:

- Don't use images that do not truthfully represent the video. In other words, don't "trick for a click". Use an image that clearly represents what the video is about, and what will be seen in the video

- Use your face if you can, and if it makes sense for your channel. Connecting with a clear image of eyes, emotion, and excitement (the three Es) is a great way to immediately connect on a human level with your viewers.
- Use text in your thumbnail, but only a few words so that it is legible at the small size that appears in the main search results and on the recommended videos section in the YouTube sidebar.
- Use a consistent style, whether that's a logo, or a color border, or a style of text, or whatever works for you and your brand.

Video Creators does an excellent job at implementing all of these strategies:

Titles, Descriptions, and Tags

These are the most critical aspects of optimizing your videos on YouTube because they are directly responsible for search ranking and placement in the first 24 hours of posting your video.

Titles

Tim Schmoyer from Video Creators says that one of the most important things to think about is your video titles and that he tries to pitch the value instead of just explain what the video is.

For instance, instead of using "How to se-up two-factor authentication on YouTube" you might say "How to prevent hackers from taking over your YouTube channel"

Here are a few things to consider prior to crafting a title for every video you upload to your channel:

- Put your focus keyword (what you'd like to rank for) at the beginning, at least within the first 4-5 words of the title.
- Do not be deceptive, especially if it's not 100% relevant to what your video is about. That will just annoy your viewers and send them away, possibly for good.

- Tease what's in the video to pique curiosity without giving it away 100%
- Test different types of titles to see what works with your audience like messing around with CAPS, using numbers, longer, shorter. Never guess, test.
- Remember that YouTube titles have a limit of 100 characters.

Here's an entertaining but useful 2 minute video with some good YouTube video title advice:

Descriptions

With 5,000 characters you get more than enough space in your description area, and you should take full advantage of as much of that area as possible. Not only is the description area a great way to give the viewer a quick 250-500 word synopsis of your video, it will also tell Google what your video is about and help rank for your preferred search terms.

Important things to remember:

- The first 2 lines show up in Google search results along with your video thumbnail. It is important to weave your keyword into the description naturally and use any other hooks and enticing words in the beginning as well.
- A 250-500 word synopsis of your video goes a long way for both the viewer experience and YouTube to help rankings.
- Use this area for strong calls-to-action like "Subscribe" (with link), external links to your website and other social profiles.

Tags

Tags are also used to help rank your videos and the tags themselves are used to support your main keyword as well as help Google understand which videos are related so they can be recommended to viewers.

Important things to remember:

- Use your keyword and varied versions of it that viewers may search for.

- Tags have a limit of 500 characters in total.
- Use your brand name, person name and actual channel name (username at the end of your YouTUbe URL) as tags -- this helps Google with recommending more of YOUR videos as related videos.
- View your competition as well as other successful videos to see their tag strategies for ideas. You can use a free plugin for Chrome provided by vidIQ that will automatically show you the tags and other stats on any videos you're watching!

Thank you!!